What's the Difference Between a Turtle and a Tortoise?

by Trisha Speed Shaskan

illustrated by Bandelin-Dacey

PICTURE WINDOW BOOKS

a capstone imprint

Thanks to our advisers for their expertise, research, and advice:

Joe Maierhauser, President/CEO
and Terry Phillip, Curator of Reptiles
Reptile Gardens, Rapid City, South Dakota

Terry Flaherty, PhD, Professor of English
Minnesota State University, Mankato

Editor: Shelly Lyons
Designer: Matt Bruning
Art Director: Nathan Gassman
Page Production: Jane Klenk
The illustrations in this book were created with watercolor.

Photo credit: Shutterstock/siloto (handmade paper), 1 (background)
and throughout in sidebars and titlebars

Picture Window Books
151 Good Counsel Drive
P.O. Box 669
Mankato, MN 56002-0669
877-845-8392
www.capstonepub.com

Printed in the United States of America in North Mankato, Minnesota.
112010
006003R

All books published by Picture Window Books
are manufactured with paper containing at least
10 percent post-consumer waste.

Library of Congress Cataloging-in-Publication Data
Shaskan, Trisha Speed, 1973–
What's the difference between a turtle and a tortoise? / by Trisha
Speed Shaskan ; illustrated by Bandelin-Dacey.
     p. cm. — (What's the difference?)
 Includes index.
 ISBN 978-1-4048-5546-5 (library binding)
 1. Turtles—Juvenile literature. 2. Testudinidae—Juvenile
literature. I. Bandelin, Debra, ill. II. Dacey, Bob, ill. III. Title.
 QL666.C5S48 2011
 597.92—dc22
                                        2010000899

A turtle rests near the water. A tortoise walks through the hot sand. Both of these animals are reptiles. But do you know the differences between a turtle and a tortoise?

Turtles spend much of their time in water. They live everywhere except Antarctica. Most turtles make their homes in hot, wet areas. But some of them live in cooler climates.

Tortoises live on land. They make their homes in dry areas. These animals are found everywhere around the world, except Australia and Antarctica.

5

Turtles and tortoises move in different ways. Turtles swim.
Most of them have webbed feet to help push their bodies
through water. But a sea turtle's front legs are flippers.
The flippers allow the turtle to cruise through the water.

flippers

A tortoise travels on land. It has to raise its heavy body and shell off the ground. Its back legs are thick and strong. A tortoise's feet look like elephant feet. The animal uses its feet to walk on or dig into the dirt.

A tortoise's legs and shell are very strong. Some large tortoises can carry a human.

Can you imagine having a skeleton on the outside of your body? Turtles and tortoises do—it's their shell. A shell protects the animals' insides.

A turtle's shell is lightweight, so the animal can swim fast. The shell is covered in large scales called scutes. Some shells are flat. Others are curved.

scute

A tortoise's shell is also covered in scutes. But the shell is large and heavy. Most tortoise shells are high and rounded.

scute

Shells are used for protection from other animals.
Some turtles and tortoises pull their heads, legs,
and tails inside their shells. They hide from enemies.
Others simply tuck their heads inside their shells.

10

When a turtle pulls its head and legs into its shell, the air in its lungs is forced out. This action makes a hissing sound.

11

Turtles and tortoises have lungs. But their ribs are attached to their shells, so breathing is done only with muscles. The animals use muscles to breathe in a gas called oxygen. Then the muscles push out the air from the lungs.

Some freshwater and sea turtles use their mouths, throats, or tails to draw in oxygen from water. Soft-shelled turtles take in oxygen through their skin.

Soft-shelled turtles have shells made of leathery skin. Their shells are not covered in scutes.

Most turtles are omnivores. They eat both plants and animals. Fish, snails, insects, grasses, flowers, and fruit are all turtle foods. Some turtles, such as the leatherback turtle, are carnivores. They eat only other animals, such as jellyfish.

Most tortoises are herbivores. They eat plants. Tortoises are slow. They would have a difficult time catching other animals to eat.

Turtles and tortoises have beaklike mouths with no teeth. They use the sharp edges of their "beaks" to bite down on food.

Like all reptiles, turtles and tortoises are cold-blooded. Their body temperature changes with their surroundings. To warm their bodies, turtles leave the water to lie in the sunshine. During cold winter months, some turtles stay underwater.

During hibernation, turtles and tortoises don't eat. They also don't take in much oxygen.

Other turtles and tortoises will dig themselves underground to hibernate. When the air warms, they go above ground.

Tortoises living in hot areas hide beneath the surface to keep cool.

Most turtles and tortoises prepare to have their young in spring. Male turtles look for female turtles. Some turtles, such as sea turtles, mate while floating in water. Others mate on land.

Tortoises also mate in spring. But tortoises mate only on land.

Male gopher tortoises fight one another to win over a female. They run into each other, trying to flip over the other.

gopher tortoises

19

After mating, all female turtles and tortoises find a place on land to lay eggs. A sea turtle digs her nest and lays her eggs on a beach.

The bigger the turtle, the more eggs it lays. A small wood turtle lays eight to 12 eggs. But a large sea turtle can lay more than 100 eggs!

20

A tortoise digs her nest in the dirt. Then she carefully lays her eggs in the nest.

Turtle and tortoise mothers cover their nests with sand or dirt to protect the eggs. They leave their eggs and never come back. After two or three months, tiny turtles and tortoises hatch from the eggs.

21

Turtle

scute

lightweight shell

beaklike mouth

flippers or webbed feet

lives in water and on land

Tortoise

heavy, rounded shell

scute

lives on land

beaklike mouth

strong back leg

Fun Facts

Turtles and tortoises can be small or big. A bog turtle is less than 5 inches (12.7 centimeters) long. A leatherback sea turtle can be 8 feet (2 meters) long and weigh 1,800 pounds (817 kilograms)!

Large sea turtles and some tortoises can live to be more than 150 years old. Tortoises on the Galápagos Islands are famous for their old age.

People are some of the biggest hunters of turtles and tortoises. People sell the animals' meat, shells, skin, and eggs.

A tortoise is so great at storing food and water that it can go for up to one year without eating or drinking.

Sea turtles look like they're crying when laying eggs. Stories say it's because they're sad to leave their eggs. But the truth is the tears help the turtles get rid of the extra salt inside their bodies.

Glossary

carnivore—an animal that eats only meat

climate—the usual weather in a place

cold-blooded—having a body temperature that changes with the surroundings

flipper—a flat limb with bones on a sea animal; flippers help sea turtles swim

herbivore—an animal that eats only plants

hibernate—to spend winter in a deep sleep

hibernation—a period of time during winter spent in a deep sleep

mate—to join together to produce young

omnivore—an animal that eats both meat and plants

oxygen—a colorless gas in the air that living things need to breathe

reptile—a cold-blooded animal that breathes air and has a backbone; most reptiles lay eggs and have scaly skin

scute—a thin, flat piece of keratin on a turtle's or tortoise's shell

skeleton—the bones that support and protect an animal's body

webbed—having folded skin or tissue that connects the toes

To Learn More

More Books to Read

Glaser, Jason. *Sea Turtles*. World of Reptiles. Mankato, Minn.: Capstone Press, 2006.

Hatkoff, Isabella, Craig Hatkoff, and Paula Kahumbu. *Owen & Mzee: The True Story of a Remarkable Friendship*. New York: Scholastic Press, 2006.

Rebman, Renèe C. *Turtles and Tortoises*. Animals, Animals. New York: Marshall Cavendish Benchmark, 2007.

Internet Sites

FactHound offers a safe, fun way to find Internet sites related to this book. All of the sites on FactHound have been researched by our staff.

Here's all you do:

Visit *www.facthound.com*

FactHound will fetch the best sites for you!

Index

Look for all the books in the *What's the Difference?* series:

What's the Difference Between a Butterfly and a Moth?

What's the Difference Between a Dolphin and a Porpoise?

What's the Difference Between a Frog and a Toad?

What's the Difference Between a Leopard and a Cheetah?

What's the Difference Between an Alligator and a Crocodile?

What's the Difference Between a Turtle and a Tortoise?